50
DECADENT FUDGE RECIPES

BY

BRENDA VAN NIEKERK

ISBN-13:978-1500587901
ISBN-10:1500587907

TABLE OF CONTENTS

TRADITIONAL FUDGE

VANILLA FUDGE

INGREDIENTS

1060 ml sugar
125 g margarine
250 ml milk
25 ml syrup
397 g condensed milk
5 ml vanilla extract

METHOD

Dissolve the sugar and the margarine in the milk.

Add the syrup and the condensed milk.

Boil, stirring occasionally until "soft ball" stage.

Add the vanilla extract and remove from the heat.

Beat until creamy.

Pour into a greased tin and allow fudge to cool, before cutting into squares.

CHOCOLATE FUDGE

INGREDIENTS

400 g sugar
45 ml cocoa powder
30 ml syrup
160 ml cream
30 g butter
2 ml salt
5 ml vanilla extract

METHOD

Combine the sugar, cocoa, syrup, cream, butter and salt.

Stir over low heat until the sugar has dissolved.

Cover until it starts boiling.

Uncover the saucepan and boil rapidly until "soft ball" stage is reached.

Cool without stirring.

Add vanilla extract and beat until creamy.

Pour into a greased tin and allow fudge to cool, before cutting into squares.

GERMAN CHOCOLATE FUDGE

INGREDIENTS

2 cups chocolate chips
12 squares of German sweet chocolate
7 oz marshmallow crème
4 ½ cups white sugar
2 tablespoons butter
1 can evaporated milk
1/8 teaspoon salt
2 cups pecan nuts, chopped

METHOD

Combine chocolate chips, German sweet chocolate and marshmallow crème in large bowl.

Combine sugar, butter, evaporated milk and salt in heavy skillet.

Bring to a boil over medium heat.

Cook for 6 minutes, stirring constantly.

Pour hot syrup over chocolate mixture.

Stir with wooden spoon until smooth.

Stir in pecans.

Spread into buttered pan.

Let stand until firm; cut into squares.

BUTTERSCOTCH FUDGE

INGREDIENTS

¼ cup butter
¾ cup sour cream
1 cup sugar
 teaspoon vanilla extract
¼ teaspoon salt
½ cup nuts
1 cup brown sugar
2 tablespoon white syrup

METHOD

Melt butter.

Add brown sugar and heat to boiling.

Add white sugar, sour cream and salt.

Cook to 236 degrees or until the "soft ball" stage is reached.

Cool the fudge mixture.

Add vanilla and nuts then beat until thick.

Pour into buttered pan.

CHOCOLATE AND GINGER FUDGE

INGREDIENTS

900 g sugar
55 g cocoa powder
500 ml milk
2 tablespoons glucose powder
115 g butter
85 g crystallized ginger, chopped

METHOD

Blend together the sugar and cocoa.

Stir in the milk.

Dissolve the sugar over a low heat.

Add the glucose and butter and bring to boil, stirring all the time.

Boil gently until "soft ball" stage is reached (116 degrees C or 240 degrees F)

This will take approximately 1 hour.

Take off the heat, add the ginger and beat the mixture until creamy.

Pour into a greased tin and allow fudge to cool

Cut into squares.

CHOCOLATE AND CHERRY FUDGE

INGREDIENTS

125 g glace cherries
125 g plain chocolate
375 g sugar
125 g honey
150 ml milk
125 g butter

METHOD

Cut the cherries in half and rinse under the cold tap.

Dry well.

Break chocolate into small pieces and put into a saucepan.

Add sugar, honey, milk and butter.

Stir over gentle heat and cook until "soft ball" stage is reached.

Take off heat and cool slightly.

Beat until thick and creamy.

Stir in cherries.

Pour into a greased tin and allow fudge to cool, before cutting into squares.

COFFEE AND CHERRY FUDGE

INGREDIENTS

300 ml evaporated milk
300 ml water
180 g butter
1 kg sugar
10 ml coffee powder
2 ml vanilla extract
100 g glace cherries, chopped

METHOD

In a large saucepan, heat milk, water, butter and sugar until sugar has dissolved.

Bring to the boil, boil rapidly, stirring occasionally until "soft ball" stage is reached (115 degrees C).

Remove from heat.

Mix coffee powder with the vanilla extract and add to the fudge mixture.

Add the cherries.

Beat the mixture until thick and creamy.

Pour into a greased tin and allow fudge to cool, before cutting into squares.

CHOCOLATE ALMOND FUDGE

INGREDIENTS

4 cups white sugar
7 oz jar marshmallow crème
1 can evaporated milk
1 tablespoon butter
2 cups chocolate chips
7 oz milk chocolate pieces
1 teaspoon vanilla extract
¾ cup almonds

METHOD

Chop and toast the almonds.

Stir together the sugar, marshmallow crème, evaporated milk and butter in a saucepan.

Cook, stirring constantly, until the mixture boils rapidly.

Boil, stirring constantly for 7 minutes.

Remove the mixture from the heat.

Add chocolate chips and candy pieces, stirring until the chocolate is melted and the mixture is smooth.

Stir in the vanilla extract and almonds.

Pour mixture into a greased pan.

Allow the fudge to set and cut into squares.

CHOCOLATE NUT FUDGE

INGREDIENTS

1 medium orange
500 g sugar
150 ml evaporated milk
125 g butter
15 ml syrup
185 g chocolate
1 small egg white
155 g mixed chopped nuts

METHOD

Grate the rind from the orange and put into a saucepan.

Add the juice from the orange to the saucepan.

Add the sugar, evaporated milk, butter, syrup and chocolate.

Stir over gentle heat until "soft ball" stage is reached.

Take pan off heat and cool slightly.

Beat until thick and creamy.

Pour into greased pan.

Leave until half set, cut into cubes.

Roll each cube into a ball.

Lightly whisk the egg white and coat each piece of fudge.

Roll the ball in the chopped nuts.

MILK FUDGE WITH NUTS

INGREDIENTS

125 ml milk
750 ml sugar
2 ml vanilla extract
2 ml baking powder
100 g chopped walnuts

METHOD

Combine milk, sugar, vanilla extract and baking powder in a wok.

Bring to boil.

Continue boiling over medium heat until thickened, stirring occasionally.

Once mixture has thickened stir continuously until the mixture separates when a spoon is drawn through it.

Remove from the heat.

Cool fudge slightly, beat vigorously until the mixture stiffens.

Add the nuts.

Pour into a greased tin and allow fudge to cool, before cutting into squares.

RICH DUTCH FUDGE

INGREDIENTS

400 g sugar
45 g butter
45 ml syrup
1 can condensed milk
Pinch of salt
1 teaspoon vanilla extract

METHOD

Melt sugar, butter and syrup over a low heat.

When all sugar grains have dissolved, add condensed milk slowly, stirring continuously.

Boil for 10 to 15 minutes.

Stir the fudge mixture, add salt and vanilla extract.

Beat lightly until creamy.

Pour into a greased tin and allow fudge to cool, before cutting into squares.

CHOCOLATE SOUR CREAM FUDGE

INGREDIENTS

500 ml sugar
250 ml sour cream
60 g dark chocolate
2 ml salt
25 ml liquid glucose
30 g butter
5 ml vanilla extract
50 g hazel nuts, chopped and roasted

METHOD

In a large, heavy based saucepan, combine sugar, cream, chocolate, salt and liquid glucose.

Stir over low heat until sugar has dissolved and chocolate melts.

Bring to boil, reduce heat, simmer, covered for 3 minutes.

Uncover and cook, stirring frequently until "soft ball" stage is reached (118 degrees C).

Remove from the heat, stir in butter and vanilla extract.

Allow fudge to cool to lukewarm without stirring.

Beat vigorously with a wooden spoon.

Stir in nuts.

Pour into a greased tin and allow fudge to cool, before cutting into squares.

COCONUT RUM FUDGE

INGREDIENTS

3 cups sugar
1 ¼ cups milk
¼ cup corn syrup
2 tablespoons butter
2 teaspoon coconut extract
2 teaspoon rum extract
Desiccated coconut

METHOD

Combine the sugar, milk, corn syrup and butter.

Cook over medium heat, stirring until mixture comes to a boil.

Cook to 238F on a candy thermometer or until "soft ball" stage is reached.

Do not stir the fudge mixture.

Remove the mixture from the heat.

Do not stir.

Cool the fudge to 120F.

Add coconut and rum extract.

Beat the mixture until smooth.

Pour the fudge into a greased pan.

Allow the fudge to set and cut into squares.

ORANGE FUDGE

INGREDIENTS

900 ml castor sugar
250 ml evaporated milk
115 g margarine
4 tablespoons orange juice
Grated rind of ½ orange

METHOD

Place the sugar and milk in a saucepan; heat very slowly until the sugar has dissolved.

Add the butter and orange juice.

Bring to boil and boil gently until "soft ball" stage has been reached (144 degrees C or 238 degrees F).

Stir occasionally during the cooking process.

Remove from the heat and cool slightly, add the rind and beat until creamy.

Pour into a greased tin and allow fudge to cool, before cutting into squares.

ESPRESSO FUDGE

INGREDIENTS

15 chocolate wafer cookies
¼ cup espresso granules
1 ½ cups sugar
½ cup margarine
5 oz evaporated milk
8 oz vanilla candy coating
7 oz jar marshmallow cream
½ cup chopped hazelnuts
1 teaspoon vanilla extract

METHOD

Blend the cookies and 2 tablespoons espresso granules until they are fine.

Combine the remaining 2 tablespoons espresso granules, sugar, ½ cup butter, and milk in a saucepan.

Cook over low heat until sugar and espresso granules dissolve, stirring occasionally. Bring to a boil over medium heat, stirring constantly.

Boil 5 minutes, stirring constantly, until mixture reaches "soft ball" stage or the candy thermometer reaches 234°.

Remove the fudge mixture from the heat.

Add the candy coating and marshmallow cream.

Stir until the candy coating melts.

Stir in hazelnuts and vanilla.

Add the reserved cookie crumb mixture creating a speckled effect.

Spread mixture into a greased pan.

Allow setting and cutting into squares.

MAPLE FUDGE

INGREDIENTS

1 ½ cups sugar
2/3 cup evaporated milk
2 tablespoons margarine
¼ teaspoon salt
2 cups chopped marshmallows
2 cups white chocolate chips
½ cup chopped walnuts
1 ½ teaspoons maple flavoring
48 walnut halves or pieces

METHOD

Combine butter, evaporated milk, sugar and salt in medium, heavy-duty saucepan.

Bring to a full rolling boil over medium heat, stirring constantly.

Boil, stirring constantly, for 4 ½ to 5 minutes.

Remove from heat.

Stir in marshmallows, morsels, nuts and maple flavoring.

Stir vigorously for 1 minute until marshmallows are melted.

Pour into prepared baking pan.

On top of fudge, place nut halves in rows spacing about 1/2 inch apart.

Press into fudge; refrigerate until firm, cut into squares.

BRANDY FUDGE

INGREDIENTS

3 cups sugar
2/3 cup milk
2/3 cup cream
¼ cup light corn syrup
2 tablespoon butter
6 tablespoons brandy

METHOD

Combine the sugar, milk, cream, corn syrup and butter.

Cook over medium heat, stirring until the mixture comes to a boil.

Cook until the "soft ball" stage is reached or until 238F on the candy thermometer.

Do not stir the mixture.

Remove the mixture from heat.

Do not stir the mixture.

Cool the fudge mixture to 120F.

Add the brandy.

Beat until mixture starts to lose its gloss.

Pour the fudge into a greased pan.

Allow the fudge to set and cut into squares.

EASY MILK FUDGE

INGREDIENTS

2 tablespoons butter
2/3 cup evaporated milk
1 ½ cup sugar
¼ teaspoon salt
2 cups chopped marshmallows
1 ½ chocolate chips
1 teaspoon vanilla extract
½ cup chopped pecan nuts

METHOD

Combine the butter, evaporated milk, sugar and salt in a saucepan.

Bring to a boil over medium heat, stirring constantly, boil for 4 to 5 minutes.

Add the marshmallows, chocolate, vanilla extract and pecan nuts.

Stir the fudge vigorously for 1 minute.

Pour the fudge into a greased pan.

Allow setting and cutting into squares.

CLOTTED CREAM FUDGE

INGREDIENTS

10 oz sugar
3½ oz golden syrup
8 oz clotted cream
½ teaspoon vanilla extract

METHOD

Place all the ingredients in a saucepan and heat gently, stirring until sugar dissolves.

Bring to the boil, cover the saucepan and boil for 3 minutes.

Uncover and continue to boil until the temperature reaches 116 °C / 240 °F or "soft ball" stage is reached.

Remove the fudge from the heat and beat until the mixture becomes thick and creamy.

Pour into a greased pan.

Allow setting and then cutting into squares.

DATE AND NUT FUDGE

INGREDIENTS

90 g compressed dates
60 g walnuts
500 g sugar
15 ml syrup
150 ml evaporated milk
A few drops vanilla extract
60 g butter

METHOD

Roughly chop the dates and the walnuts.

Place the sugar, syrup, evaporated milk, vanilla and butter into a saucepan.

Stir over heat until the sugar has dissolved.

Boil the fudge mixture to "soft ball" stage.

Take off heat and cool slightly.

Beat until thick and creamy.

Stir in 2/3 of chopped dates and nuts.

Pour into a greased pan.

Add the rest of the dates and nuts on top of the fudge mixture.

Allow setting and cutting into squares.

WHISKY FUDGE

INGREDIENTS

3 cups sugar
2/3 cup milk
2/3 cup cream
¼ cup light corn syrup
2 tablespoons butter
6 tablespoons whisky

METHOD

Combine the sugar, milk, cream, corn syrup and butter.

Cook while stirring until mixture comes to a boil.

Boil until "soft ball" stage is reached, approximately 238F on candy thermometer.

Do not stir.

Remove the fudge from the heat.

Do not stir the fudge mixture.

Cool to 120F.

Add whiskey.

Beat until mixture starts to lose its gloss.

Quickly pour into greased pan.

STRAWBERRY FUDGE

INGREDIENTS

2 tablespoons lemon juice
12 oz evaporated milk
3 cups white sugar
2 tablespoons butter
1 ¾ cups sliced fresh strawberries

METHOD

Combine the milk, sugar and butter in a saucepan.

Boil the mixture.

Stir in the strawberries and lemon juice.

Boil the mixture stirring constantly until "soft ball" stage is reached, between 234 and 240 degrees F (112 to 116 degrees C).

Remove from heat and quickly pour in a greased pan.

Allow setting before cutting into squares.

CHOCOLATE PEANUT BUTTER FUDGE

INGREDIENTS

3 cups white sugar
1 cup evaporated milk
¼ cup cocoa powder
½ cup peanut butter
1 tablespoon butter

METHOD

Combine the sugar, evaporated milk and cocoa powder into a saucepan.

Stir over a high heat until the mixture comes to boiling point.

Lower the heat and continue the cooking until a "soft ball" stage is reached.

Remove the fudge from heat.

Add the peanut butter and margarine.

Beat until the fudge is creamy.

Pour into a greased pan.

Allow to cool and cut into squares.

CHOCOLATE BUTTERSCOTCH FUDGE

INGREDIENTS

1 cup sugar
15 oz condensed milk
½ cup water
6 oz chocolate pieces
6 oz butterscotch pieces
¼ cup butter
1 teaspoon vanilla extract
1 cup chopped walnuts

METHOD

Combine the sugar, condensed milk, water, chocolate and butterscotch pieces in a saucepan.

Cook stirring constantly until the "soft ball" stage is reached, about 234F on a sugar thermometer.

Remove the mixture from the heat.

Combine the butter and vanilla extract.

Pour the hot mixture into the bowl.

Beat until the mixture starts to thicken.

Add the walnuts.

Pour into a greased pan.

Allow setting and cutting into squares.

APPLESAUCE FUDGE

INGREDIENTS

1 cup applesauce
6 oz butter
2/3 cup evaporated milk
Pinch salt
3 cups sugar
2 cups marshmallow cream
1 teaspoon vanilla extract
1 cup icing sugar
2 teaspoon apple pie spice
1/2 cups chopped and toasted pecan nuts

METHOD

Place the applesauce, butter, evaporated milk, salt, and granulated sugar in a saucepan over medium-high heat and bring to a boil, stirring constantly.

Cook, stirring constantly to prevent scorching, until it reaches 235 degrees F or the "softball" stage.

Remove the saucepan from the heat and stir in the marshmallow cream, vanilla extract, icing sugar, apple pie spice and pecan nuts.

Stir until all ingredients are blended.

Pour the fudge into the greased pan.

Allow setting and cutting the fudge into squares

PINEAPPLE FUDGE

INGREDIENTS

700 g castor sugar
85 g butter
250 ml evaporated milk
250 ml water
85 g crystallized pineapple

METHOD

Chop the crystallized pineapple in pieces.

Place the sugar, milk, butter and water into a saucepan.

Dissolve the sugar over a low heat.

Add the glucose and butter and bring to boil, stirring all the time.

Boil gently until "soft ball" stage is reached (116 degrees C or 240 degrees F)

Take off the heat.

Add the pineapple and beat the mixture until creamy.

Pour into a greased pan.

Allow fudge to cool, before cutting into squares.

LEMON AND WHITE CHOCOLATE FUDGE

INGREDIENTS

150g white chocolate chips
3 cups sugar
2 tbsp light corn syrup
1¼ cups milk
4 tablespoons butter
1 teaspoon lemon extract

METHOD

Melt chocolate in pan over very low heat.

Stir in sugar, corn syrup and milk.

Cook while stirring until the sugar dissolves.

Cook the mixture to the "softball" stage or 238F on a thermometer.

Remove from heat, and without stirring, add butter.

Cool the mixture to 120F.

Add the lemon extract and beat until mixture begins to thicken.

Pour the mixture into a greased pan.

Allow setting and cutting into squares.

HONEY FUDGE

INGREDIENTS

30 ml honey
30 g margarine
210 g icing sugar
125 ml boiling water
1 egg white
5 ml vanilla extract
Chopped walnuts

METHOD

Combine honey, margarine, icing sugar and water into a saucepan.

Stir the mixture until sugar has dissolved.

Boil rapidly until the "soft ball" stage is reached.

Beat the egg white until stiff peaks are formed.

Pour over the hot mixture, beating constantly.

Add the vanilla extract.

Beat until mixture is firm enough to keep it's shape when dropped by spoonfuls onto a waxed paper.

Press half a walnut into each piece of fudge.

Allow the fudge balls to dry overnight.

KAHLUA FUDGE

INGREDIENTS

1 1/3c ups sugar
7 oz marshmallow crème
2/3 up evaporated milk
¼ cup butter
¼ cup Kahlua
¼ teaspoon salt
2 cups chocolate pieces
1 cup chocolate pieces
2/3 cup nuts, chopped
1 teaspoon vanilla extract

METHOD

Combine the sugar, marshmallow crème, milk, butter, Kahlua and salt in a saucepan.

Boil rapidly while stirring constantly for 5 minutes.

Remove the mixture from the heat.

Add all the chocolate.

Stir the mixture until melted.

Add the nuts and the vanilla extract.

Turn into prepared pan.

Allow the fudge to set and cut into squares.

IRISH CREAM FUDGE

INGREDIENTS

1 cup walnuts
4 cups sugar
1 cup evaporated milk
1/3 cup corn syrup
6 tablespoons margarine
2 tablespoons honey
½ teaspoon salt
½ cup Irish Cream liqueur
½ cups chocolate chips

METHOD

Chop the walnuts.

Combine the sugar, evaporated milk, corn syrup, butter, honey, and salt and cook over a medium-low heat, stirring constantly until sugar dissolves.

Do not stir while syrup is boiling.

Cook until syrup reaches the "soft ball" stage, approximately 234 to 240 degrees F.

Add the liqueur to syrup; but do not stir until syrup cools.

Add the chocolate and beat fudge until it is no longer glossy and thickens.

Pour the fudge mixture over the nuts.

Allow the fudge to cool completely and then cut into squares.

DARK CHOCOLATE FUDGE

INGREDIENTS

3 cups chocolate chips
14 oz. condensed milk
Pinch of salt
1 cup chopped walnuts
1½ teaspoon vanilla extract

METHOD

Melt the chocolate chips together with the condensed milk and salt.

Remove the saucepan from the heat.

Mix in the walnuts and the vanilla extract.

Spread into a greased pan.

Allow fudge to set and cut into squares.

COOKIE AND
UNCOOKED FUDGE

FUDGE SQUARES

INGREDIENTS

250 g butter
500 g icing sugar
2 eggs
1 teaspoon vanilla extract
225 g crushed cookies

METHOD

Beat the eggs.
Melt the butter in a saucepan.
Stir in the icing sugar.
Cool for 1 minute.
Blend the eggs and vanilla extract into the mixture.
Add the crushed cookies.
Press into a greased pan.
Allow the fudge to set and then cut into squares.

CREAM CHEESE FUDGE

INGREDIENTS

3 oz cream cheese
1 teaspoon cream
2 cups icing sugar
2 oz melted chocolate
½ teaspoon vanilla extract
1 pinch salt
1 cup assorted, chopped nuts

METHOD

Beat the cream cheese and cream until smooth and well blended.

Gradually beat in the sugar.

Add the melted chocolate.

Stir in the vanilla extract, salt, and chopped nuts.

Press into a greased pan.

Allow setting and cutting in squares.

CHOCOLATE MINT FUDGE

INGREDIENTS

2 cups milk chocolate chips
14 oz condensed milk
2 teaspoons vanilla extract
6 oz white chocolate chips
1 tablespoon peppermint extract

METHOD

Melt the milk chocolate chips together with 1 cup of condensed milk.

Add the vanilla extract.

Pour half the chocolate mixture into a greased pan.

Allow the pan to chill for 10 minutes.

Keep the remaining chocolate mixture at room temperature (melted).

Melt the white chocolate chips with 1 cup of condensed milk.

Add the peppermint extract.

Spread the white chocolate mixture over the chilled chocolate layer.

Chill the pan for another 10 minutes.

Spread the reserved chocolate mixture on mint chocolate layer.

Allow the fudge to set and then cut into squares.

UNCOOKED NUTTY CHOCOLATE FUDGE

INGREDIENTS

225 g chocolate
100 g butter
1 egg
450 g sugar
30 ml condensed milk
5 ml vanilla extract
50 g walnuts, finely chopped

METHOD

Beat the egg.

Melt the chocolate and butter together in a bowl over hot water.

Mix the egg, sugar, condensed milk and vanilla extract together.

Blend the egg mixture into the chocolate mixture.

Add the nuts.

Pour the mixture into a greased pan.

Allow fudge to set and cut into squares.

UNCOOKED CHOCOLATE FUDGE

INGREDIENTS

4 squares chocolate
¼ butter
1 lb icing sugar
¼ cup condensed milk
1 egg
1 teaspoon vanilla extract
Chopped, assorted nuts

METHOD

Melt the chocolate and butter together in a saucepan.

Add the icing sugar, condensed milk, egg and vanilla extract.

Mix together until well blended.

Add the chopped nuts.

Put the mixture into a greased pan.

Allow fudge to set and cut into squares.

OREO COOKIE FUDGE

INGREDIENTS

170 g white chocolate
300 ml condensed milk
2 cups crushed Oreo cookies

METHOD

Melt the chocolate and the milk in a saucepan.

Remove the chocolate from the heat and stir in the crushed Oreo cookies.

Pour into a greased pan.

Chill until set and cut into squares.

FABULOUS FUDGE

INGREDIENTS

3 packets of chocolate chips
½ lb margarine
10 oz chopped marshmallows
2 cups chopped, assorted nuts
4½ cups sugar
1 can evaporated milk
1 tablespoon vanilla extract

METHOD

Combine the chocolate chips, butter, marshmallows and nuts.

Blend the sugar with the evaporated milk and boil for 6 minutes.

Remove from the heat and add vanilla extract.

Pour the milk mixture into the bowl with first four ingredients and stir until well blended.

Pour into a greased pan.

Allow setting and cutting into squares.

WHITE CHRISTMAS FUDGE

INGREDIENTS

500 g sugar
397 g condensed milk
75 g butter
100 g marshmallows
350 g broken white chocolate
100 g chopped pecan nuts
100 g chopped glace cherries

METHOD

Cut marshmallows into small pieces.

Place sugar, condensed milk less 50 ml and butter into a saucepan.

Bring the mixture to boil all the while stirring constantly.

Boil the mixture for 5 minutes.

Remove from the heat and stir in the marshmallows, chocolate, nuts and cherries.

Stir until chocolate has melted.

Stir in remaining condensed milk.

Press the dry crumbly mixture into a greased pan.

Allow the fudge to set and cut into squares.

CHOCOLATE FRUIT FUDGE

INGREDIENTS

25 ml cocoa powder
50 ml coconut
25 ml sultanas
25 ml cornflakes
25 ml cookie crumbs
50 ml condensed milk
5 ml sherry
25 ml chopped nuts

METHOD

Crumb the cornflakes into fine crumbs.

Combine all the ingredients except for the chocolate.

Mix the mixture well.

Press into a greased pan.

Melt the chocolate over hot water and spread over the fruit mixture.

Refrigerate until set then cut into squares.

CREAMY MOCHA FUDGE

INGREDIENTS

½ cup cocoa powder
3 ½ cup icing sugar
¼ cup cream
½ cup butter
2 tablespoons strong coffee
½ cup chopped pecan nuts

METHOD

Stir the cocoa powder and the icing sugar together.

Melt the butter over a medium heat.

Add the coffee and beat until smooth.

Mix in the pecan nuts.

Pour the mixture into a greased pan.

Refrigerate till set then cut into squares.

TRIPLE CHOCOLATE FUDGE

INGREDIENTS

3 1/3 cup sugar
1 cup butter
1 cup dark brown sugar
12 oz evaporated milk
1 oz baking chocolate chopped
1 teaspoon vanilla extract
32 large marshmallows cut into halves
2 cups chocolate chips
14 oz milk chocolate candy bars, broken 2 squares
2 cups chopped pecan nuts

METHOD

Combine the sugar, butter, brown sugar and evaporated milk.

Cook and stir over medium heat until sugar is dissolved.

Bring to a rapid boil and boil for 5 minutes, stirring constantly.

Remove from the heat and stir in marshmallows until melted.

Add chocolate chips and stir until melted.

Add chocolate bars and baking chocolate and stir until melted.

Blend in the vanilla extract and pecan nuts.

Pour into a greased pan.

Chill until firm and cut into squares.

MICROWAVE FUDGE RECIPES

CREAMY FUDGE

INGREDIENTS

393 g condensed milk
50 g icing sugar
12.5 ml margarine
5 ml vanilla extract
3 ml chocolate or brown coloring

METHOD

Place the condensed milk and icing sugar in a glass bowl.

Microwave on high for 8 to 10 minutes.

Stir in the margarine, vanilla extract and coloring into the mixture.

Pour into a greased pan.

Allow fudge to cool and then cut into squares.

DOUBLE CHOCOLATE FUDGE

INGREDIENTS

14 oz. condensed milk
12 oz. chocolate chips
1 oz dark chocolate
1 teaspoon vanilla extract
1 ½ cup assorted chopped nuts

METHOD

Place the milk, chocolate chips and chocolate into a glass bowl.

Mix the mixture well.

Microwave the mixture uncovered on high (100%) for 1 minute.

Stir the mixture.

Microwave until chocolate is melted and mixture can be stirred smooth (for about 2 minutes).

Stir in the vanilla extract and the nuts.

Spread the mixture evenly into a greased pan.

Refrigerate until firm and cut into squares.

WHITE CHOCOLATE FUDGE

INGREDIENTS

> 500 g icing sugar
> 100 g white chocolate
> 50 ml milk
> 10 ml rum essence
> 100 g margarine
> 125 ml chopped dried fruit and nuts

METHOD

Place all the ingredients except the nuts and fruit into a glass bowl.

Place in a microwave and microwave on high for 2 minutes.

Stir the mixture well.

Microwave for another 2 minutes.

Stir the mixture again for a second time.

Microwave for another 1 minute in the microwave.

Add the fruit and nuts and blend into fudge mixture.

Pour the mixture into a greased pan.

Allow fudge to cool before cutting into squares.

PISTACHIO FUDGE

INGREDIENTS

3 oz. cream cheese
14 oz.condensed milk
½ teaspoon vanilla extract
18 oz. chocolate chips
1 tablespoon butter
½ cup pistachio nuts

METHOD

Coarsely chop the pistachio nuts.

Place cream cheese in glass bowl.

Microwave the cream cheese on HIGH (100%) 15 to 25 seconds or until cream cheese has softened.

Add 2 tablespoons condensed milk and the vanilla extract.

Beat on until mixture is smooth.

Place the remaining condensed milk, chocolate and butter in glass bowl.

Microwave on medium (50%) 2 to 3 1/2 minutes or until mixture can be stirred smooth.

Mix in the pistachio nuts.

Spread the chocolate mixture evenly into the greased pan.

Pour cream cheese mixture over chocolate mixture.

Swirl lightly over the chocolate mixture to create a marble effect. Chill and then cut into squares.

MARSHMALLOW FUDGE

INGREDIENTS

2 cups miniature marshmallows or chopped up
large marshmallows
14 oz. condensed milk
1 pinch salt
12 oz. chocolate chips
1 cup milk chocolate chips
½ cup nuts
1 ½ teaspoon vanilla extract

METHOD

Combine the marshmallows, milk, and salt.

Place in a microwave and microwave on HIGH 3-4 minutes.

Stir the mixture until the marshmallows melt and mixture
is smooth.

Add the chocolate chips and stir until melted.

Stir in the nuts and vanilla extract.

Spread the mixture evenly in a greased pan.

Chill before cutting into squares.

MICROWAVE CHOCOLATE FUDGE

INGREDIENTS

4 cups icing sugar
½ cup cocoa powder
¼ cup milk
½ cup butter
2 teaspoons vanilla extract

METHOD

Blend the icing sugar and cocoa powder together.

Pour the milk over the mixture and add the butter.

Do not mix the mixture.

Place in a microwave and microwave until butter is melted, takes approximately 2 minutes.

Stir in vanilla extract and stir vigorously until the mixture is smooth.

Pour the mixture into a greased pan.

Chill before cutting into squares.

PEANUT BUTTER FUDGE

INGREDIENTS

12 oz. chocolate chips
12 oz. peanut butter
14 oz. condensed milk

METHOD

Melt the chocolate and peanut butter on high power for 3 minutes in a microwave (make sure you use a heat resistant bowl).

Stir the mixture well.

Add the milk and stir until the mixture is well blended.

Pour the mixture into a greased pan.

Refrigerate to chill before cutting into squares.

COCONUT FUDGE BALLS

INGREDIENTS

2/3 cup evaporated milk
2 ½ cups icing sugar
12 oz. chocolate chips
1 cup chopped assorted nuts
Coconut to roll the fudge balls in

METHOD

Blend the chocolate bits and milk, place in microwave and microwave until melted. Takes about 3 minutes.

Stir the sugar and nuts into the melted chocolate.

Chill the mixture for about ½ hour.

Form the mixture into balls.

Color the coconut and roll the balls in the coconut.

20287656R00036

Printed in Great Britain
by Amazon